# New Horizons

International Business
and Emerging Markets

Kevin Griffiths MSc

Copyright © 2012 Kevin Griffiths

All rights reserved.

ISBN: 1480044814
ISBN-13:978-1480044814

# DEDICATION

Without any doubt I would have never completed this paper without the support and encouragement of my wife Franciska. A big thank you to you and our children Rebecca, Lucas, Victoria, Cassandra, Olivia, Noah and Isabella for giving me the time, space , understanding and love needed to complete this task. Your sacrifice does not go unappreciated.

Thanks also to The University of Liverpool and Laureate Education who provided the motivation and resources for me to complete this work during my studies for a MSc in International Management.

ACKNOWLEDGMENTS

Thanks also to The University of Liverpool and Laureate Education who provided the motivation and resources for me to complete this work during my studies for a MSc in International Management.

# 1

# The international business environment.

## Globalization Development

The delivery of the globalization dream is full of conflicting concepts and political exploitation. International commercial interests in terms of market penetration and competitive advantage development are influenced in outcome by not only commercial decisions but political manipulation and in some cases corruption. To say that globalization is a route out of poverty for developing countries could be argued on a very basic level, however, commercially driven strategies where profit is king will lead to exploitation and manipulation of the poor and disenfranchised in the developing countries. The utopian believe that global free trade will lead to greater wealth distribution and high living standards is lost and unachievable while political interference and exploitation prevail. We can see examples of states enhancing their development within Europe e.g Spain and Ireland mostly generated by political will, economic enhancements and infrastructure subsidies from the EU rather than pure commercial sense and resource availability in a free trade environment. These advantages of commercial incentives and infrastructure subsidies are not so available to third world developing countries. In the areas of manufacturing the opportunity for exploitation in developing countries is greatest, and, we have seen this with the exposure of several western brands use of sweatshops and child exploitation.

Taking on board the pitfalls and exploitative potential of globalization it is important to recognise and develop the advantages that can become available for all organisations, countries and individuals. We are all in an interconnected world and with the ever increasing rates of technological expansion the opportunity to integrate culturally and commercially sensitive organisational expansion is key to overcoming poverty and allowing individual enhancement. With globalization comes social and cultural responsibility.

Recent examples of rapid growth in developing countries are now being exposed to rapid decline because the bases of growth was exploitation and not sustainable development. For globalization to succeed in developing countries it must focus on sustainable development. The full implementation of a free global economy must be developed on commercial equality and not inequality, although Lindert and Williamson (2001) argue "the source of that inequality would be poor government and non-democracy in those lagging countries, not globalization" This may be true but business and politics, hence governments, exist and operate in unison. Although Cook and Kirkpatrick (1995) point out "there continues to be a general skepticism regarding the capacity of government to intervene in a manner that will improve overall well-being."

Examples of successful integration by organisations can in fact be misleading if we look at the city of Bangalore in India, a city perceived as a modern thriving environment built on the establishment of international technology companies. Madon (1997) highlights several issues of concern around the internationalization of employment including rampant wage increases, infrastructure deficiencies including power shortages as the city tries to deal with rapid expansion. While we can see elements of benefit in the establishment of new business in poor undeveloped areas it must be understood that if the wealth generation is not channelled in to social development and gain then the divergence between rich and poor will grow and conflict and instability will ensue.

Technological development is a good example of injecting economic growth in to an area but as Madon (1997) highlights "There is an evident tension between the notions of entering the global information society and local development." For successful globalization we must look further than the balance sheet and look in to effecting sustainable social gain and cultural integration.

**New Ventures**

Globalised economy structures and the freeing up of currency restrictions is an ideal environment for the establishment of INV's for new and emerging organisations. The very nature of small start up operations, innovative adaptability and market penetration flexibility are best suited to creating competitive advantage globally. Traditional established organisations expanding into new international ventures face more implementation issues such as organisational cultural trends and restrictive internal bureaucratic practices that may be unable to adapt to new market cultures.

To successfully establish an INV there are several elements and criteria that have been identified as being key factors, entrepreneurship, resourcefulness and adaptability. These factors have been evaluated and established as fundamentals to success. While these established fundamentals are recognized it is also an important part of project criteria to highlight that the concept of organisational structural fluidity to meet the specific requirements of the operating environment. A system more appropriate to young emerging organisations than established leviathans.

New technological advances have created

opportunity for young and new organisations to penetrate larger global markets. As Oviatt & McDougall (1993) highlight global start ups may be more difficult than domestic based, although they do seem to show a more sustainable market position. With new operations the impact of little resource availability means the outsourcing of services specific to the cultural and social environments add to the customization of market penetration and allows for faster competitive advantage to be established. This was identified by Oviatt & McDougall (1993)

Oviatt & McDougall (1994) lay down the theories of INV which have the bases for successful integration for new ventures in an international context. When identifying attributes for success they highlight resourcefulness and entrepreneurship as key elements. These elements will allow young vibrant companies to assimilate and expand in diverse cultural markets. Unlike large top heavy corporations entering a new international arena. In fact as Oviatt & McDougall (1994) state the size of the organisation is not the focus but the age. Newer fresher organisations focusing specifically on entering the international arena are more capable of achieving competitive advantage because of their evolutionary and adaptable approaches.

When entering new markets on an international level it is vital to maintain control and monitor activities in a variance of marketplaces. This concept was pointed out by Oviatt & McDougall (1994) "Their emphasis on controlling rather than owning assets is due to resource scarcity that is common among new organizations." This ability to establish non owned assets and resources while imposing control is a critical force in developing and maintaining competitive advantage. Organizations that fit and apply the principles of entrepreneurship and resourcefulness will find a smoother entry process and faster acquisition of competitive advantage.

We operate in an expanding and demanding environment that requires fast responsive actions to develop and maintain competitive advantage in the international market place. The advantage of new companies to allocate and identify resources and implementation plans suitable in a range of environments simultaneously is a critical component of success.

There may be times when size and experience will play a major role in market penetration within specific sectors but generally youth and flexibility are an advantage especially within the realm of technology based service industries.

As Zahara (2003) concluded that Oviatt & McDougall (1994) have started an important and influential research stream, whose contributions have been insightful, powerful and varied." It should be recognized that while these observations are an important part of assessing INV's we must keep evaluating and developing mechanisms of market entry to challenge existing market leaders.

In conclusion we can assume that the findings and theories of Oviatt & McDougall (1993) and supported by Zahra (2005) are a valid assessment of the requirements for INV's.

2

# Foreign direct investment and the multinational enterprise.

## Investment Benefit

Engagement in FDI for corporations is driven by the seeking of competitive advantage, and, for recipient countries the motivation can be seen as social and local economic gain, especially within the developing economies.

In a global economy FDI plays a significant role in furthering the concept of globalization and to a certain extent the social enhancement of the recipient country. however, the political ramifications of this process can have an adverse effect on both the investor and host country. While these factors play a role in deciding the nature of FDI for corporations the overwhelming factor will be the identification of potential competitive advantage.

Whether the FDI is horizontal or vertical there are going to be issues that will need to be addressed in relation to PR and the perceived impact at home and at the host country. The closure of plants in one country and transfer to another will have varying negative impacts for the organisation and government in one country and an opposite positive potential in the new country.

The drive by host countries to develop FDI potential has resulted in the creation of Bilateral Investment Treaties (BIT's). These treaties are designed to balance the rights of foreign investor with the host countries domestic investors. While these treaties may go some way in assuring potential investors there appears to be only a slim connection between BIT's and FDI as concluded by Tobin & Rose-Ackerman (2003) "BIT's appear to be important instruments for riskier countries that wish to attract FDI, but, in general, they may not fulfill their major objective" Although BIT's may not show a significant increase in FDI it does show that firms need to be secure in their investment and that the stability and legal structure of the host country is going to impact on the decision to invest.

With the need to grow and develop markets the advantages for firms to expand into new geographic areas for the achievement of greater market targets and production advantage is a reality of globalization We have seen major car manufactures moving and developing manufacturing plants on a global scale to obtain competitive advantage in differing target markets.

FDI seems to offer positive advantages for firms providing there is security of investment, As de Mello Jr (1999) identifies that providing the following factors are accounted for, Political risk, policy structure, trade regime and institutional structure , then FDI can offer advantages for firms. FDI plays a role in the economic development of a host country concluded by Carkovik and Levine ( n.d ) "there is a positive link between FDI and growth." FDI is a necessary part of globalization, no matter what advantages and benefits host countries receive the driving influence will be the security and return for investing corporations in terms of profit and competitive advantage.

# 3

# Environments of international business.

**Asset stripping or sustainable growth? - The FDI question.**

Issues around the benefits of governments generating employment through subsidy incentives to foreign corporations and investors is a contentious matter in many quarters. The returns to the economic output of the country should show that the return on the subsidy outweighs the initial subsidy, however, governments do not necessarily offer and operate on the basis of financial return. Social and political advantage will go a long way to justify government expenditure. When issues of unemployment are concerned the motivation for governments to be seen as "doing something" means that political payback may play a major role in inward investment strategy. With the closure of coal mines in Wales during the eighties the drive for inward investment and job creation played a significant part in regenerating areas affected by the mine closure. This regeneration involved a move to service industries like call centre operations and technology based assembly units, this provided relieve to a population that was facing high unemployment but did nothing to establish a long-term sustainable economy. When the going got tough and subsidies reduce the corporations left. FDI is an exploitative program that asset strips the local communities.

Haskel et al (2007) assessment using ARD and ONS data may reflect more biased and incomplete data because of the governments needs to justify its FDI strategy. While ARD and ONS are independent there will always be questions on data supportive of government policy. Although the balances and awareness of bias have been accounted for at various stages of investigation one should be aware that bias adjustment may well create bias.

Statistical assessment of bigger economic issues that are driven by political will and social development may not reflect true economic advantage to FDI on the host nation while the true winner is the corporation receiving the subsidy and market advantages from attracting government departments.

Applying FDI as a means of gaining political advantage has been questioned by Phelps & Tewdwr- Jones (2001)"It is noteworthy just how much prestige has been and continues to be placed on inward investments by RDAs and the government as flagship economic development projects when compared to support for indigenous firms." How government promote FDI to there public seems to ignore the true economic situation as pointed out by Haskel et al (2007) "the per-job value of spillovers are less than per-job incentives governments have granted in recent high-profile cases." This could be seen as evident with the government encouragement of foreign car manufacturers to replace the demised home spun car manufacturing industry.

Inward investment has been used as a tool to alleviate social unrest and dissatisfaction of government economic policy is a concern that to a certain degree is addressed by Haskel et al (2007) while collecting data "The first and most important is to reiterate that these calculations are only suggestive, as they rely on many assumptions and caveats." The assumptions around returns from subsidy input show that even with the limited information FDI is not profitable for governments who instigate subsidy. For FDI to achieve benefit for its host it must be operationally sustainable without the creation of an artificial reality through the "propping up" strategy of promoting FDI through uncompetitive government support. The research and its underlying nature confirms my view that within the UK FDI was a politically motivated act that did not show any advantageous elements to the long-term economic stability of the nation.

4

# Environments of international business.

**Cultural Environment**

Inward investment within a country can face cultural barriers in the initial stages of development. There will always be social questions around the motivation of the MNE's that settle in areas of social deprivation. Questions by some of the community around motivations of foreign companies and possible different ways of dealing with management - worker relations.

During the eighties in Wales there was a massive reduction and closure of the mining industry and a highly unprofitable state owned steel industry. The result was a high level of unemployment and social unrest. There was a policy of attracting FDI to replace the lost industries, however, the available workforce was mainly manual and the trend was to create low skill employment environments Huggins (2001) "only 14% of newly located plants had a workforce already in

place that was sufficiently highly skilled for the plants' particular needs", that resulted in up skilling opportunities and vocational training programmes. From a cultural and historical point there was a collective awareness of previous foreign exploitation from the English industrialist. Any investor would be wise to accommodate the fears and concerns of the community. In fact with larger Japanese, Korean and other Asian countries, investing heavily in assembly factories, managed to reduce these fears and establish good management - worker practices not possible with the previous structures around unionization Education plays a significant role in establishing a MNE in a new host country in relation to the communities perception.

Investing in an area that has suffered

exploitation require careful and sensitive management. By offering educational packages and encouraging up-skilling and skill shifting opportunities companies and communities bonded. Huggins (2001) "It was found that the large majority of foreign-owned plants in Wales (88%) have utilized aftercare training and skills development initiatives"

There is also a tendency towards a lack of local commercial development that means there are opportunities for MNE's to develop new operations in relatively competitive free environment. Calkins & Wiener (1998) "Welsh agencies agree that cultural as well as structural values have impeded the development of indigenous industry."

Korean company LG became a major investor in Wales in 1996 by promising to create 6100 jobs for an investment of £1.7billion. Although the was a skill mismatch in the area, education mechanisms where embedded into the community to assist the companies development. Phelps et al (1998) identify that as a result of this FDI A semiconductor training centre was established and local universities provided industry specific degrees. All of this was a result of significant government grants and subsidies made to LG and training agencies.

Short comings in social and cultural environments should not be a barrier to investment. Where there is a skill shortage training and corporate development can play a major part in establishing and integrating new MNE's into Wales as seen by the LG example . Unfortunately this is not always the case and it has resulted in the lack of spillover advantage and entrepreneurial development. By educating and encouraging the workforce the MNE will establish a more sustainable and innovative presence within the country.

**Stable strategy with a third leg.**

When an organisation enters a new foreign market it is faced with many structural and strategic issues. Traditionally companies faced resource and market penetration issues for successful activity, however, one area that was regarded as a secondary issue was that of the institutional bodies that directly and indirectly accommodate the commercial functionality of the state and industry. There needs to be a greater understanding of the local legal, political and social environment for MNE's to sustainably enter new foreign areas of operation.

As Peng et al (2008) point out "Institutions are much more than background conditions" They go on to say that institutions directly influence the strategy of an organisation to help create competitive advantage. This competitive advantage is only achievable in a sustainable way when strategies placate local institutions and communities. This could be seen as being more crucial in emerging and developing economies where free market approaches are new and not fully understood. The concept of creating a tripod strategy that takes into account Competition, Resources and Institutions seems a sound system for succeeding in the effective establishment of a new organisational presence within a new market.

**(1) Anti dumping as entry barriers;**

Peng et al (2008) examines four areas that take into account the need to accommodate the assessment and inclusion of institutional mechanisms within any developed strategy. Each area explores the mechanisms of controlling MNE's into participating within the cultural, social and economic environments of the host.

Anti dumping legislation can be used as a method of protectionism by the host country, while there may be cases of attempted market manipulation by market entrees, the exploitation of the law can be prohibitive of free trade. It is imperative for the MNE to fully understand the impact of there market entry on local companies and their relationship and communication mechanisms with local and national institutions. Peng et al (2008) quoting (Schuler et al., ( 2002) were right to assume that "when industry- and resource-based weapons fail, there is a direct implication for domestic firms under competitive pressures from imports: An institution-based view of international business strategy launch an institution-based missile by filing an antidumping petition ".The use of an institution as a means of reaching or maintaining competitive advantage is a counter productive strategy that can have greater negative impact on future trading partnerships.

## (2) Competing in and out of India;

If we look at India then we see the negative

issues of success. When institutions successfully implement strategies that enable local companies use local resources to develop products and services that become global powerhouses then external institutions will embark on limiting or even prohibiting market entry for that nation and establish restrictions in outbound FDI. Understanding that institutions are fluid and mechanisms of control and policies are not always consistent or permanent. While openness increases growth opportunity it can be exploited when success needs to be controlled.

### (3) Growing the firm in China;

When institution mechanisms are poor then there opportunities for interpersonal networking structures to informally establish protocols can be seen in China, this maybe a cultural development but may well evolve into more formal institutional organisations that will impact on future trade development. In fact Peng et al (2008) recognise that market entrants will need to establish links with the informal inter-organisational bodies "as evidenced by the numerous international strategic alliances with local firms" Understanding and communicating with local structures is paramount to successful market entry, however, as local markets and organisation evolve it is vital that MNE's keep the fingers on the pulse of local political and legal activity.

## (4) Governing the corporation in emerging economies.

Corporate governance may well operate effectively within modern trading organisations comfortable with, and adapted to, dispersed ownership. However, New and emerging economies may find the concept difficult and alien. The concept of singular or minority control of an organisation that shows little or no transparency will tend to be the norm in emerging markets. The difficulty will arise primarily arise between principles of the organisation. I tend to agree with Peng et al (2008) who cite Morck et al.,(2005); Young et al., (2008) that "In emerging economies, governance reforms need to find ways to reduce (certainly not increase!) such concentrated shareholding in the hands of controlling shareholders" Failure to enact a more transparent and open policy on governance will on hinder emerging organisations and host nations.

Peng et al (2008) highlight the importance in assimilating the policies, laws and social treats of local venues for MNE's. It becomes imperative the there is an harmonious relationship between corporations and institutions. This relationship will promote understanding and enhance the development and enactment of strategies within the operating market.

In relation to governmental or local interference to protect local interests one can assume that this will yield short term political advantage, but eventually leads to reduced economic activity that inhibits globalization and free trade. It is almost a requirement for MNE's to take on board the issues as seen by local and national institutions.

5

# Global integration and international finance.

## Financial Crisis

Financial mechanisms employed on the global markets are the communicators of institutional and organisational policies and strategies. The current situation is a reflection of poor political and managerial understanding or corrupt self motivated and miss managed regulation of commercial financial institutions around the world. While many see the origins of the the current crisis as being manifested because of the sub prime lending policies, especially within the banking institutions of the United States. These actions where carried out through greed motivation of banking staff and poor and ineffective control systems by regulatory bodies and governments. As Reinhart & Roghoff (2008) point out factors behind the crisis "It also follows a well-trodden path laid down by centuries of financial folly."

The result of this miss management as resulted in the slowing of national economies and a majority of businesses on a global scale, resulting in increases in unemployment, reduced borrowing opportunities for emerging and developing organisations. The social implications will reflect on government policy which may not result in the most sensible long-term solutions. The political desire to be seen to do something with a short term positive result will only help increase votes for the ruling party and may not result in a stable and sustainable economy. We have seen the scenario of boom and bust many times and all of this is predominantly driven for short term political gain.

The concept of free trade becomes challenged when home countries see the activities of other nations being able to produce products more efficiently because this effects in a negative manner the output of domestic product. This will result in the political institutions introducing trade restricting and blocking rules to help domestic organisations, with the result that retaliatory actions are then instigated, resulting a more downward and restricted global economy. Although during the current crisis there has been a verbal resistance to trade restrictions in the traditional sense, nations are moving back to the concept of 'Buy products produced here'. This could be seen has a form of restrictive manipulation to trade.

When faced with financial crisis the stabilization of markets becomes the paramount concern of controlling institutions. In this particular case the need to heavily support and in some cases nationalize and underwrite banks has in itself created some uncertainty. This uncertainty will require the application of new, more responsible and stronger regulatory mechanisms on local, national and international levels. As Taylor (2008) concludes "Most urgently it is important to

reinstate or establish a set of principles to follow to prevent misguided actions and interventions

in the future" .It could be argued that if you remove the commercial profit term from the banking sector and replace it with a developmental motivation under control of national governments it would help reduces the future risks of damage to economies. An alternative would be to establish banks along the lines of the Credit Union movement and remove the profit motivation and high incentives.

The current crisis highlights the short comings of the current global financial institutions. To enable a truly global economy that fully exploits free trade there will need to be a radical rethink of how these institutions act and relate to governments. Free trade can only be damaged by the global financial sensitivity that has been demonstrated by both the Asian and Global crises. The emerging economies will become more economically interrelated with established markets and more vulnerable to the historical financial and economic cycles. This was highlighted by Fidrmuc & Korhonen (2009) "the global economy may be moving to a situation characterized by increasing interdependencies between developed and emerging economies." To be in a position of global financial stability we must overhaul and adapt our trading and regulatory systems.

## Contagion Crisis

The concept of financial contagion as an explanation of reactions and situational fiscal positioning is explored in relation to the Mexican, Asian and Russian crises. The assumption that financial linkages to a country undergoing financial crisis contribute to higher probability of cross border crisis expansion is explored. It seems a logical assumption that the knock on effects of a crisis will manifest in commercially and economically related organisations and institutions. This symbiotic bonding of currencies and financial relationships play a significant role in the regional interpretation and implementation of future fiscal strategies at all levels of trade. The understanding of the fundamental causes of crisis transmission will allow for more effective management and prevention of future negative financial events.

Investors looking on a regional basis need to make judgements on the cause and effect scenarios related to a particular situation to fully benefit from crisis situations. While the argument from Caramazza et al (2004) that "The common creditor is the most important and significant variable"

it is not going to be the only factor to

accommodate in investor reactionary strategy to a financial crisis. While the general concept would be a process of damage limitation on the part of the investor which may involve withdrawal thus impacting, potentially, on deepening the crisis. as a result of knee jerk reactions from investors as Caramazza et al (2004) point out "some countries, therefore, may experience capital outflows"

The assessment of empirical evidence by Caramazza et al (2004) focusing on the Identifying Crisis, Measuring the common creditor and their importance along with the Implied probability of crisis and Robustness goes towards understanding the inter relationships of financial processes and reactions. The implication that no one factor is instrumental to crisis transmission we must understand that perceptions to crisis as well as factual interpretation will factor into investor reactions.

The assumption that common creditor is key to financial contagion is based on current commercial interpretation mechanisms. Building on the understanding of the interpretation systems and their effects on cross border transmission will allow us to rethink and modify the standard response mechanisms employed by investors today and allow for the development of more sustainable and stable financial and currency transactions. Thus, helping stabilize economic environments.

The methods employed by Caramazza et al (2004) face the situation in a way that removes the original country. This may allow for knock on assessment but by not allowing for additional internal cause factors e.g political and perceptive positions, the true picture may not be fully visible. To fully understand contagion we must look deeper and wider for a true and consolidated position on the intricacies of international cross border financial evolution.

Concluding that situations in one financial environment will impact on surrounding financial environments is a fair and correct assumption, however, we must not view situations in a segmented and independent manner. Like most things in live the bigger picture can give better clues to the reactionary situations, it is the detail that we can be lost in and miss the whole picture and the most effective reactions. Caramazza et al (2004) conclusions may well be valid in their terms of reference but not in relation to the bigger picture of the three crises they were evaluating.

The concept of contagion is assessed in different ways and there fore the concept needs to be standardized for a fuller academic and comparative assessment. Kaminsky & Reinhart (1998) "contagion has been understood to be different things across different studies" Transmission of financial disease is not to be viewed in isolation there are many factors that may well increase and decrease it 's progress, including social and political environments.

# 6

# International business strategies.

## Strategy Operations

Starbucks have successfully and rapidly entered the international arena with a tactically aggressive expansion programme. The venturing into and sustaining a global operation requires flexibility and innovation. The process of developing and sustaining strategies that are, or potentially, diverse requires a significant amount of organisational cultural tolerance and understanding. identifying an appropriate national strategy that compliments the fundamentals of the parent company is a key strategical process. Deciding on the method of entering and timing of entry into a particular market will be the key drivers in whether the organisation gains competitive advantage.

Maximizing on market place opportunities and identifying key players and potential partners would be a major element when reviewing potential markets.

When markets become saturated organisations need to look for new operating environments. Gupta and Govindarajan (2000)"Today, globalization is no longer an option but a strategic imperative for all but the smallest firms" There are many criteria involved in developing a new customer sectors and globalization offers opportunities to many companies. Even for organisations trading in many countries the development of new country markets may well offer new tactical and cultural issues. Over coming this issues will form the basis of the 'introduction strategy' development. One approach would be in the identification of modes of entry that benefit from local experience. By developing relationships with local players the company can gain significant advantage. The fundamentals of entry can be identified as Location, timing and mode of market entry. The successful analysis of these factors could well determine the level of commercial success.

The successful identification of a partner for

entry is going to be one of the key steps, next it is to look at the structure of that partnership. Deciding on partnerships, licensing or franchising will depend among other things on the commitment of both parties and the cultural environment being entered. The Starbucks entry strategy is identified by Dutta and Subhadra (N.D) "Starbucks decided to enter international markets by using a three pronged strategy:Joint Ventures, Licensing and wholly owned subsidies" There are many risks associated with international markets such as

Operational, Political, country, technological and Environmental (Dutta and Subhadra (N.D)). By using native partnerships allows for greater understanding of the cultural trends and reactions to influencing situations. However, by diluting the shareholding the is a risk that profits will not be a complete as if a wholly owned operations was active. Dutta and Subhadra (N.D)"Analysts observed that Starbucks was unable to earn enough revenues from its international operations due to complex joint ventures and licensing agreements."

While the success of Starbucks is apparent on many street corners its future strategy in terms of international expansion will need to be reviewed. The current mechanisms work in terms of market entry but may not be sustainable through the Joint Venture or Licensing track unless there is a reworking of the agreements. The brand strength should now empower them to negotiate more favorable terms. However, it must be recognized that successful entry for Starbucks does not mean that it will be a sustainable position. They must look to regaining ownership where possible. Barkema et al (1997)"International wholly owned subsidiaries allow firms to learn how to operate in foreign settings without the complexities of cooperating with a partner"

7

# Global financial management and accounting.

## Payment Methods

The issues around trade payment security is a critical factor for MNE's. Where price margins are low there becomes increased sensitivity to currency fluctuations and guarantee payment methods. Globalization and technological advances allow for a potential seamless transfer of funds. Giovannucci ( n.d ) "As new technologies and advances in communications are changing trade logistics and speeding and facilitating transactions, businesses are finding new opportunities and new ways to operate." However, distance and detached commercial activity requires that both parties in a transaction feel secure and confident in the designated transaction process. These process' are instrumental in maintaining efficient and profitable trading.

The resources available to assist in secure international trade payments are focused on 5 key areas as highlighted by Giovannucci ( n.d ) Cash in advance, Letter of credit, Documentary collection, Open account or credit, Counter trade or Barter. There becomes a practical and strategic process in defining which mechanism is most beneficial to the organisation. Issues also around invoicing strategy also come into play, the choice of currency will play a part in ensuring a solidified value to the product being traded in terms of value assessment . Exposure to risk should be minimized by all parties although the necessities of global trade and pricing strategies may require payment options that are potentially risky for one party. This may well impact on the strategical continuance issues regarding forward pricing models for the purchaser. Accounting for potential losses due to non fulfillment of contractual obligations will be a critical part of managing the process.

Deciding on the mechanism for payment is

going to impact on pricing, in particular, relating to how and in what form/ currency is used, along ,with credit financing of larger projects. The financing through the banking system or government guarantee systems can assist MNE's to enter markets that would normally offer high risk environments. The use of such systems will as been a widely used mechanism for MNE's expansion strategies. Organizations should strategically measure the impact and consequentness of its invoicing and payment strategies to meet is production, financial and fulfillment targets. Invoicing in a specific non home currency may offer some solidity to transactions when several customers over a range of countries as highlighted by Grosse and Behrman (1992)"exchange risk assessment acquires a new dimension when operations are spread over several types of INC (International contractor) activities or in several different countries."

While there are a plethora of payment and financing options for organisations the driving factor is going to be protecting the organisation both as a purchaser and provider. Identifying the suitable vehicle for an organisations international payment and invoicing methods must play a major role in its international trading strategies. Although Hauner (2002) points out "For trade in manufactured goods between MDCs, the major part of contracts are denominated in the exporter's currency and most of the remaining contracts are denominated in the importer's currency, while third-currency invoicing is relatively rare ("Grassman's Law").I would suggest that third country currency may offer a more secure and beneficial mechanism for MNE's.

8

# Global marketing, supply chain, and human resources.

## Global Marketing

The issues for an MNE's marketing operations can vary depending on the product and the environment it is released into. It becomes critical to asses the brand in terms of language and cultural values. These issues are more problematic with the movement of established brands from one country to another. Many marketing complications can be more readily addressed with new internationally focused products. The transference of products into a new market should need to fit with the strategy employed in the original market, if changes are needed to incorporate the product then an organisations marketing strategy should be locally based and focus on the cultural and social interpretation of the brand. Palich & Gomez-Mejia (1999) "one of the most important challenges organizations face is that of effectively managing cultural diversity."

Understanding the target market within a local context means that the introduction of established brands should migrate smoothly if conditions of culture and language are addressed. With globalization comes a desire from a marketing perspective to establish an almost generic process through brand standardization As Jain (1989) points out "the decision on standardization should be based on economic pay off, which includes financial performance, competitive advantage, and other aspects." We can see many products and brand with an almost universal image around the globe, however, it must recognized that this form of marketing many well work, the ability to manipulate and modify strategies to a local audience may offer better product placement and competitive advantage. Rather than going down the route of 'genetically' modifying brands to fit a global view marketeers should be adapting strategies to the environment and engendering local values and perceptions instead of global stereo typing.

The successful implementation of an international marketing strategy should recognise the cultural fluidity and diversity of the country or region the organisation is entering. Campaigns that try to establish alien concepts and values will under achieve in the short term. The embedding of a new brand that has a well established international reputation may prove easier to introduce, but for strong establishment it will still require 'localizing'

The addition of many more variables in to an international marking environment means that the marketing manager must understand a growing number of cultural, political and social conditions. While understanding the diversity of environments it also becomes important to reduce the number of conflicting points in a product introduction thus smoothing the transition from one market to another. This is highlighted by Schuiling & Kapferer (2004) "there are many reasons to encourage the development of brand portfolios that contain a balanced mix of strong local and international brands." By engaging a mix of messages it becomes easier to convey a value for a product that meets a greater audience and reduces the risk of customer isolation.

9

# Emerging issues and risks.

## E Commerce

The birth of e-commerce and internet trading could be described as the time of mass entrepreneurial rising. The empowerment of individuals and SME's in a globalized economy offers challenges to MNE's. The flexibility of smaller organisations over more cumbersome international bodies means that competitive advantage of MNE's can be more vulnerable to challenges via the internet. This new tool of communication and international trading platform offers enormous potential to all who can master its environment. In the early days of the commercialization of the web it was the forward thinking entrepreneurial organisations that became leaders in the media and it was left to the established MNE's to go through a period of catch up.

The dream of e-commerce has not been a smooth path and in fact it raise many issues for the supplier and consumer. For the supplier issues around global image and product conformity begin to play a growing part in the international marketing strategy of the organisation as raised by Lo & Kao (2008) "any e-businesses operating on the Internet have a growing international presence and cannot ignore their global marketing image." The consumer faces issues of trust and security along with assessing the credibility of the supplier. Teo &Liu (2007) "The concept of trust is crucial because it affects a number of factors essential to online transactions, including security and privacy."

Dealing with the above issues is only part of the picture faced by users of e-commerce, for effective and economic application it becomes important for the establishment of functioning and stable infrastructure. This as been recognized by many governments who are embarking on programmes to ensure that a high percentage of their population have access to fast stable internet connections. This has been a strategy employed by emerging economies such as China. Ng (2009) "A positive trend of e-commerce can assist the sustainability of growth in the country's international trade."

Today the need for an NME to have a web strategy is as vital as any other part of it organisational structure. As for the SME the NME face similar factors when entering the e-commerce field. Wilson et al (2008) "Where technology-related factors are significant, they tend to relate to skills availability rather than finance or availability of appropriate software." Over coming the technological issues and being able to resource the online presence and its required logistical support structures then offers an effective channel of sales and promotion activities for an organisations international trading.

The web has become the face or shop window of most organisations and providing there is continuing support of governments in the development and building of the infrastructure, much like the development and building of interstate highways in the USA, there will be fast economic payback.

Has we as individuals become more comfortable with online trading and feel secure in the transactions then e-commerce will continue to play a major part in the sales and product promotion of the majority of international traders.

We have seen rapid growth of e-commerce offer the last seven years and all indicators are that it will continue to grow. The way in which organisation approach their entry into this sector will have a lasting influence on their success. This is not an area that easily translates the conventional marketing approaches and requires new and customized approaches that meet and address the fears of the customer, who now has more power, influence and choice.

## ABOUT THE AUTHOR

Kevin Griffiths has over 30 years experience in developing new and emerging organisations in both the commercial and the 'not for profit' sector. He lives in Ireland and travels extensively. He has also published

**Management of Eco-tourism and its Perception: A Case Study of Belize.**

**International Management - Getting your head out of the managerial cloud.**

www.internationalmanagementbooks.com

Contact: kevin@jaffamedia.com

www.ingramcontent.com/pod-product-compliance
Lightning Source LLC
Chambersburg PA
CBHW061518180526
45171CB00001B/240